MACK WILBERG

A CLOUD OF WITNESSES

for SATB choir and piano four-hands or orchestra

text by David Warner

MUSIC DEPARTMENT

OXFORD
UNIVERSITY PRESS

OXFORD
UNIVERSITY PRESS

Great Clarendon Street, Oxford OX2 6DP,
United Kingdom

Oxford University Press is a department of the University of Oxford.
It furthers the University's objective of excellence in research, scholarship,
and education by publishing worldwide. Oxford is a registered trade mark of
Oxford University Press in the UK and in certain other countries

First published in 2020

Impression: 1

ISBN 978–0–19–353201–4

Music origination by Stephen Lamb
Text origination by Michael Durnin
Printed in Great Britain on acid-free paper by
Halstan & Co. Ltd, Amersham, Bucks

Instrumentation

The accompaniment to this work exists in two versions:

1. For piano four-hands

The pianists play from the vocal score.

2. For full orchestra

3 flutes (3rd doubling piccolo)
2 oboes
2 clarinets in A
2 bassoons
4 horns in F
2 trumpets in C
2 trombones
bass trombone
timpani (optional)
percussion 1—suspended cymbal, bass drum, chimes, glockenspiel
percussion 2—xylophone, vibraphone
harp
celeste (or keyboard)
piano
organ (if no trumpets and trombones)
strings

Full scores and instrumental parts are available on hire/rental from the publisher's Hire Library or appropriate agent.

The Tabernacle Choir and Orchestra at Temple Square have recorded this piece with orchestral accompaniment on the CD *Tree of Life: Sacred Music of Mack Wilberg* (SKU 5198840).

Composer's note

A Cloud of Witnesses weaves multiple witnessing stories of Christ's Resurrection into a single tapestry. Drawing on accounts from all four Gospel writers and the opening of the Acts of the Apostles, I have tried to convey something of the momentum of overlapping, successive stories and the breathless astonishment among Christ's followers as the reality of the Resurrection becomes clear.

To create a more panoramic and universal perspective, the piece avoids the use of soloists. Where the choir narrates the action, listeners sense that each event is a facet of a broader, more brilliant whole. And where the choir represents major characters, the audience recognizes that every 'actor' is less anachronistic and more symbolic of all human experience.

In scriptural witnessing stories, there is a clear distinction between visual recognition and spiritual understanding—between seeing and believing—a distinction that demarcates sacred and secular interpretations of the events. Throughout the work, this difference is represented musically by chant-like accounts of physical 'seeing', interspersed with more contrapuntally enriched moments as Christ's disciples come to a deeper spiritual understanding.

As one would expect, the simple, tightly circumscribed melodies of the narrative tend to be more declamatory. By contrast, the polyphonic responses—alleluias, spiritual awakenings, and Christ's own injunctions—naturally inform, enrich, and elaborate upon the narrative facts. By design, these contrapuntal nodes cluster around small, close groups of pitches, creating harmonic 'clouds' as each individual account lends form and strength to the developing 'cloud of witnesses' (a metaphor borrowed from Hebrews 12:1).

Conveying this 'cloud' in just over twenty minutes allows listeners to grasp the scope and sweep of this revelatory period. After a short instrumental dawn, the women at the empty tomb enquire frantically, 'Never shall we see him?'. Then, as the chronicle comes to an end, Christ repeats his own promise that he will continually be with those who believe. As the first words of the work are a repetition of the fear-filled 'never', the conclusion is a gentle, comforting, everlastingly sustained 'alway'.

Duration: 22 minutes

This note and the text may be reproduced as required for programme notes.

Text

The Women
Never, never shall we see him?
Never resting in his tomb?
Never, never to anoint him?
Never free of grief and gloom?
Peter, angels saw us frightened,
Knew we sought him crucified.
John, they told us, "He is risen!
Come and see where he once lay.
Go and tell he's gone before you,
Gone to Galilee this day!"

Then, how they ran—
Peter the Rock and John, beloved one—
Certain to find his body still entombed within,
John stooping down and Peter striding in.

Peter and John
Here are the linen clothes.
Here is the napkin folded, neatly laid.

What kind of thieves would here be duly
   staid
To loose this covering from his head,
And set it soft below?

Still, they saw with their eyes alone,
Doubting that he had risen,
Held captive by dread that they could be
   imprisoned;
They wept in each other's arms ·
And grieved the hour,
And mourned the day,
And rent their hearts,
And ran away.

For they knew not the scripture
That Christ must rise again.

Then Mary of Magdala
Looked into the sepulchre weeping
And saw there two angels,

As seraphim o'er the ark reaching,
Or sentinels at an empty well,
Or vessels of truth only heaven can truly tell.

The Angels
Woman, why do you weep?

Mary Magdalene
Because they have taken my Lord,
And I know not where to find him.

And turning round,
She saw a lowly gardener
Who asked the selfsame question:

The Savior
Woman, why do you weep?
Whom do you seek?

Mary Magdalene
If you've taken my Lord
(If you've hidden his body),
Where can he be found?
(For if he arises as Lazarus,
He'll come forth among wicked men
Without a friend.)

The Savior
Mary!

Mary Magdalene
Master!

And she reached out her hand,
Desiring to be nearer.

The Savior
Restrain me not, for I have not ascended
Into my Father's presence,
But go and tell my brethren I first ascend
   to him—
To my God and your God—
The Father of us one and all.

Then ponder on this witness,
This precious reminiscence:
That she who first perceived him
By hope and believing,
Received him in her grieving,

And in our sorrow we will see him
Soon appear!

Then she ran back,
Breathless, telling them
How her night of mourning
Became her joy in the morning.
Ashes to ashes—
Beauty for ashes!
But these were idle tales to those who
   doubted.

When James's mother went—Mary—
And Salome and the women,
They saw two angels sitting,
Waiting to lift the burden of their fear.

The Angels
Why are you here?
Why are you seeking him, grieving?
Why look for life where death its spoils is
   keeping?
Come see where he was sleeping,
Then go and tell he has risen,
And waits where his first draught of fish
   was given.

As the women ran to tell,
Christ greeted them with 'All hail'.
And bowing down, they worshipped him with
   joy!
Alleluia! Alleluia! Alleluia!

That day,
As two disciples left Jerusalem
In flight to the village of Emmaus,
A fellow traveler joined them by the way,
Imploring, 'Why do you walk along this road
   so sad?'
And they marveled that he was unaware.

The Two Disciples
Have you not heard that Christ
Has been condemned and crucified?
We trusted he was the one who would
   redeem all Israel.
But thieves did steal his body,
And women speak of angels!
And seeing none of it with our eyes
Can we believe it's true?

v

Good man, then what can we do but weep
And sorrow through and through?

The Savior
O ye foolish, tender children,
How slow in your hearts to believe
What prophets foretold
From Moses till now—
Remember all the scriptures saying
One should suffer even death for you!

And they drew nigh to the village,
Pleading for the stranger to tarry:

The Two Disciples
Abide with us, 'tis eventide.

And so they sat at meat, all three together.
And when he took the bread and broke it,
Even the bread of his affliction,
And he blessed and freely
Gave it unto them,
Their hearts beheld that it was Jesus—
Saw him, felt him, knew him,
And he quickly vanished!

The Two Disciples
Then it was him!
Our Lord and Master!
Jesus, Savior, our Redeemer!
Were our hearts not burning,
Souls not yearning,
Though our eyes were not discerning
Of him?

And leaving the village,
That very hour returning
To where the eleven were gathered, meeting,
These two told what had happened—
How first they misperceived him,
But breaking bread, they knew him,
And knowing, then could not see him.
Marveling thus with soft hearts opened,
Christ came among them.

The Savior
Peace be unto you.
My peace I give unto you.

Still they were all affrighted—
They thought they'd seen a ghost!
And trusting not their hearts
But eyes instead,
They yet believed but
Not for joy.

Thus, in their fearing,
The memories of his being
Were hidden from them,
And withered in them,
Until they heard him saying:

The Savior
Why are ye troubled?
What thoughts arise in your hearts?
Behold my hands,
Behold my feet,
For spirits have not this flesh—
This bone that ye see and feel me have.

Then he ate of fish before them,
Rehearsed the words of the prophets,
And calling them forth to tender his wounds,
He readied them to hear his sweet command:

The Savior
Be ye witnesses of these things!
And as God my Father sent me,
So peacefully do I send thee,
And bless thee,
And breathe on thee and say:
Receive the Holy Ghost!

But Thomas disbelieved,
For he saw not.
And since he had not beheld Christ,
What witness could he then bear?
And eight days hence, to him and more
Christ came:

The Savior
Peace be unto you.
My peace I give unto you.
Arise, come forth—
Come, Thomas, see
And feel my wounds for thee.

And reaching, Thomas witnessed,
And heard the call,

   The Savior
   Be not faithless but believing.

And feeling, believing, Thomas cried,

   Thomas
   My Lord, my God!

Away to Galilee
The erstwhile fishermen hurried,
But all night caught nothing
Until Christ called to them, 'Children!'
Then drawing in their nets
A draught was given
Which they did bring before
Their risen Lord.

   The Savior
   Peter, lovest thou me?

Their Master asked.

   Peter
   Yea, Lord, I do!

And three times Peter reassured,

   Peter
   Thou knowest I do!
   Thou knowest I do!
   Thou knowest I do!

Then came the Savior's plea:

   The Savior
   Go feed my lambs,
   Go feed my sheep!
   Go feed my sheep!

And at his call unto the mountain top
They gathered, some to worship, some yet
   doubting,
With this question in their hearts:

   The Apostles
   Is it time?
   Wilt thou now restore thy kingdom unto
      us—
   To all the House of Israel?
   Is it time?

   The Savior
   It is not for you to know what God has
      put—
   Has kept—within his holy power.
   Fear ye not!
   Ye shall yet receive his power
   When soon the Holy Ghost shall come
      upon you.
   Then, preach my word!
   Be a witness unto me in all the world!

And thus he vanished from the sight
Of their eyes,
In a cloud.
Yet still they did yearn to see
Till two angels asked,

   The Angels
   Why gaze up and grieve?
   For your Lord and Master soon will come
   As you have seen him go!

Then be ye witnesses!
A cloud of witnesses,
Who feel and know and sing
Of Christ who rose to walk with us,
To heal and comfort us,
Renew and ransom us,
Till by his grace we rise
And run with joy this blessed race,
At last to see his face!

O may our hearts receive
And evermore believe
His promise sure,
'Lo, I am with you alway'.

              David Warner
              Based on the Gospels and Acts 1,
              King James Version

for The Tabernacle Choir and Orchestra at Temple Square

A Cloud of Witnesses

David Warner
(based on the Gospels and Acts 1)

MACK WILBERG

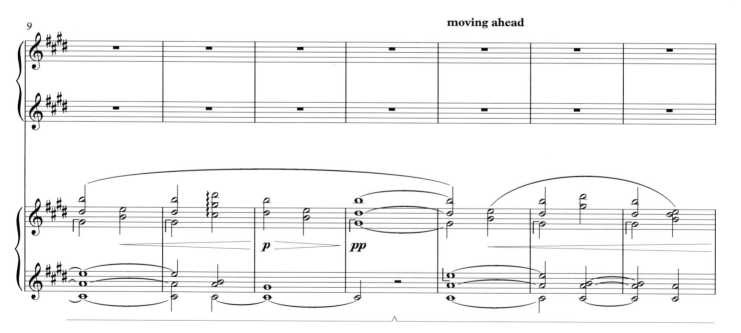

OXFORD UNIVERSITY PRESS, MUSIC DEPARTMENT, GREAT CLARENDON STREET, OXFORD OX2 6DP
The Moral Rights of the Composer and Author have been asserted. Photocopying this copyright material is ILLEGAL.

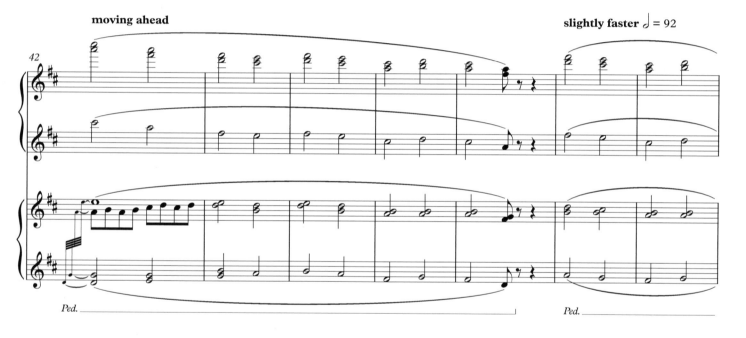

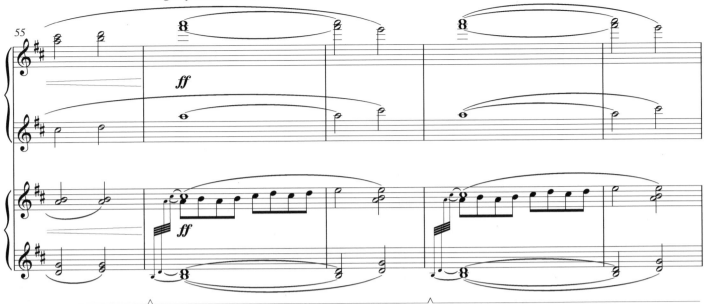

Gone! Gone! Gone to Ga - li - lee this day!'"

unis.

Gone! Gone! Gone to Ga - li - lee this day!'"

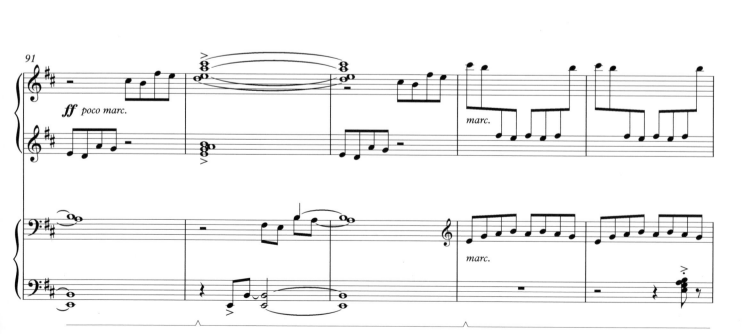

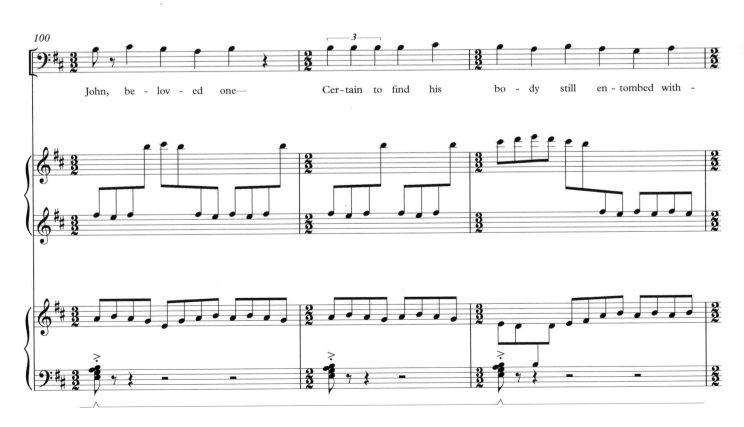

- in, John stoop - ing down and Pe - ter strid - ing in.

Ped. *Ped.* *sim.*

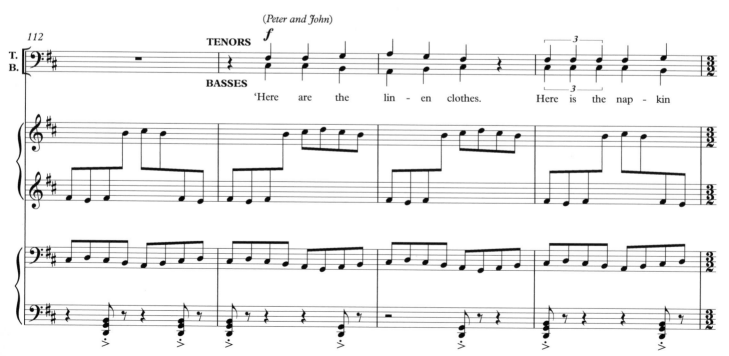

(Peter and John)
TENORS

BASSES

'Here are the lin - en clothes. Here is the nap - kin

folded, neat-ly laid. What kind of thieves would here be du-ly staid___ To

loose this co-v'ring from his head, and set it soft be-low?'

Still, they saw with their eyes a - lone, Doubt - ing that he had ris'n,

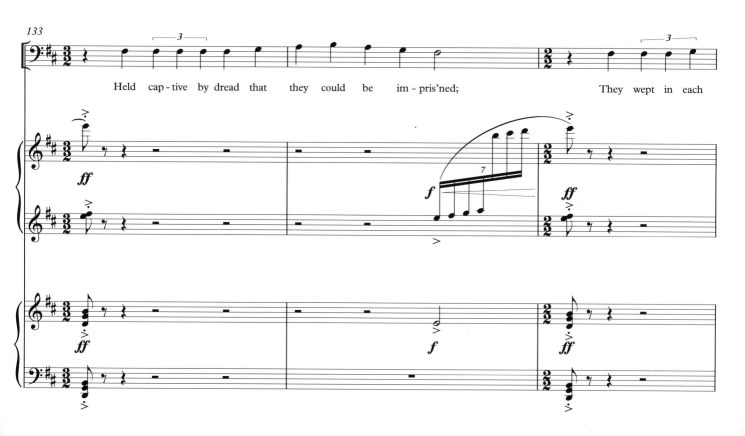

Held cap - tive by dread that they could be im - pris'ned; They wept in each

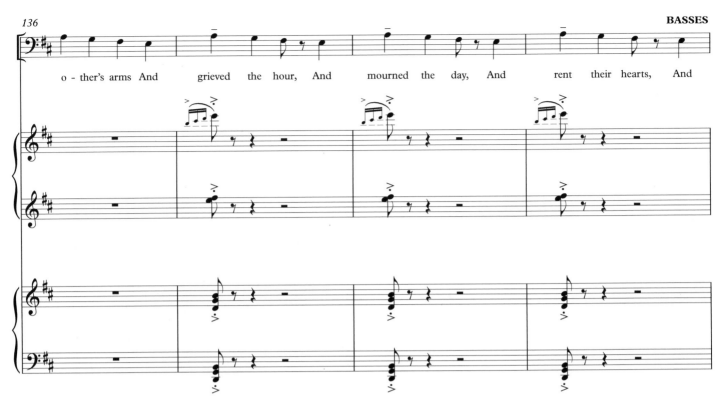

o - ther's arms And grieved the hour, And mourned the day, And rent their hearts, And

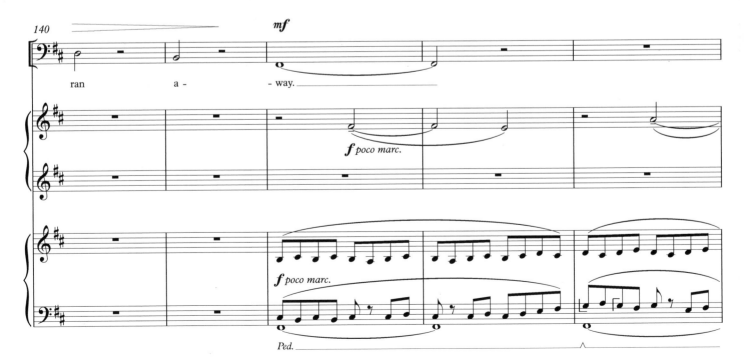

ran a - way.

TENORS & BASSES *mp* *with introspection*   **rit.**

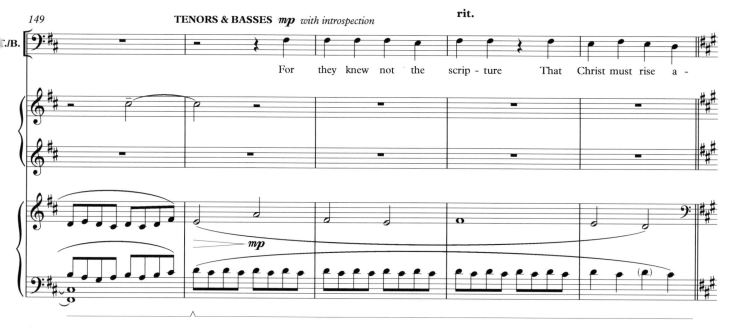

For they knew not the scrip - ture That Christ must rise a -

a tempo

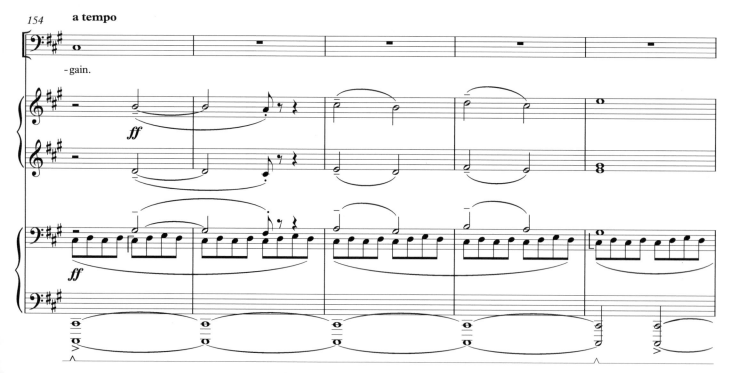

-gain.

SOPRANOS & ALTOS *unis.* *mp*

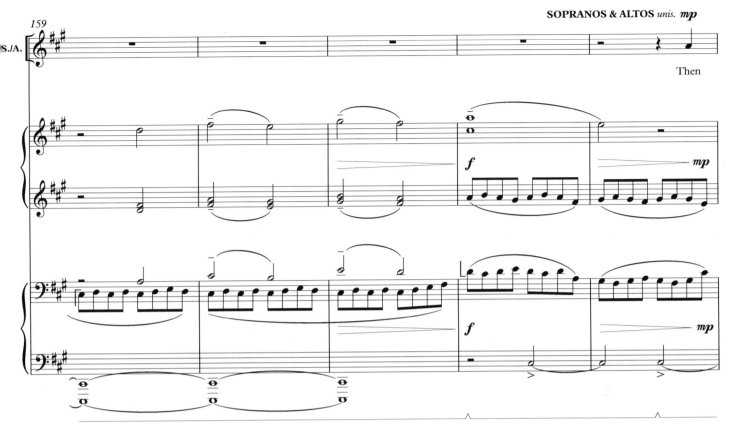

Then

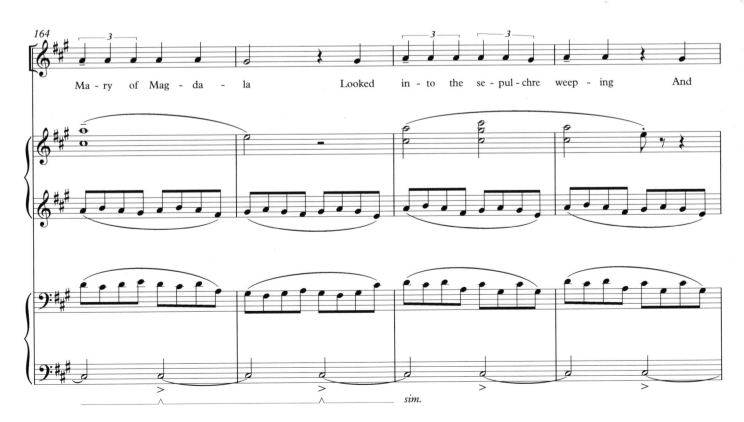

Ma - ry of Mag - da - la Looked in - to the se - pul - chre weep - ing And

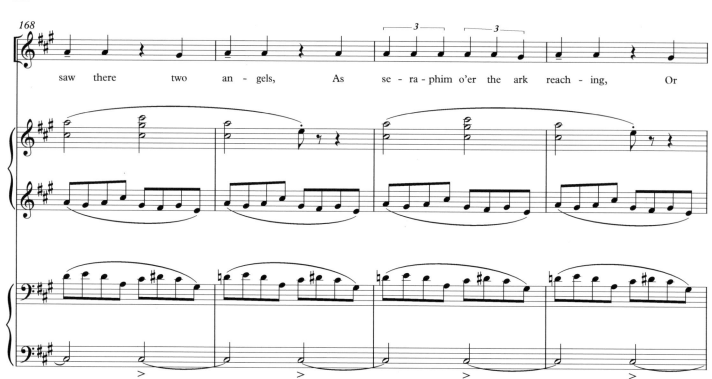

saw there two an - gels, As se - ra - phim o'er the ark reach - ing, Or

sen - ti - nels at an em - pty well, Or ves - sels of truth on - ly heav'n can tru - ly

176 **Transparent, with shimmer**

tell.

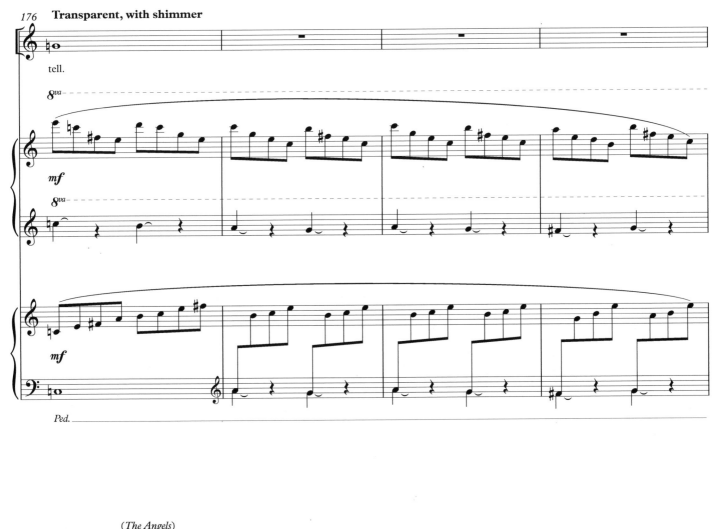

(The Angels)

180 TENORS

T.
B.

BASSES

'Wo - man, why do you weep?'

turn - ing round, She saw a low - ly gar - d'ner

Who asked the self - same ques - tion:

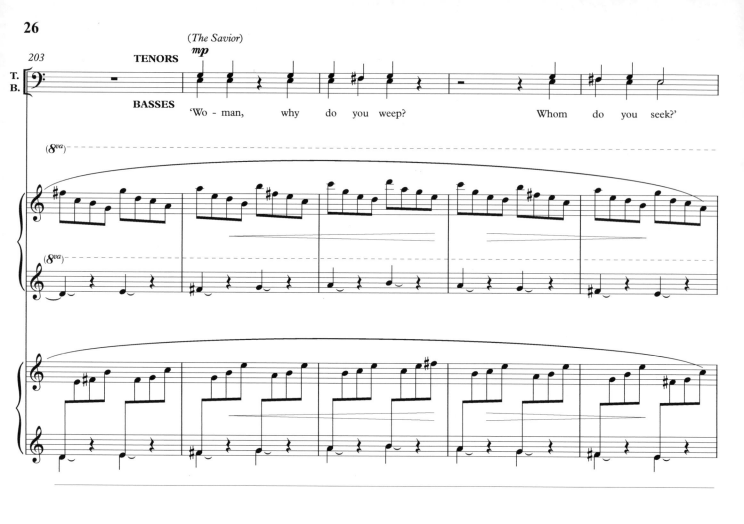

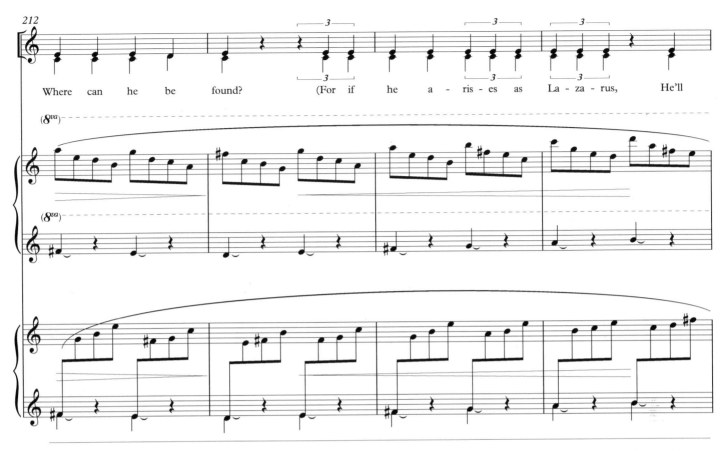

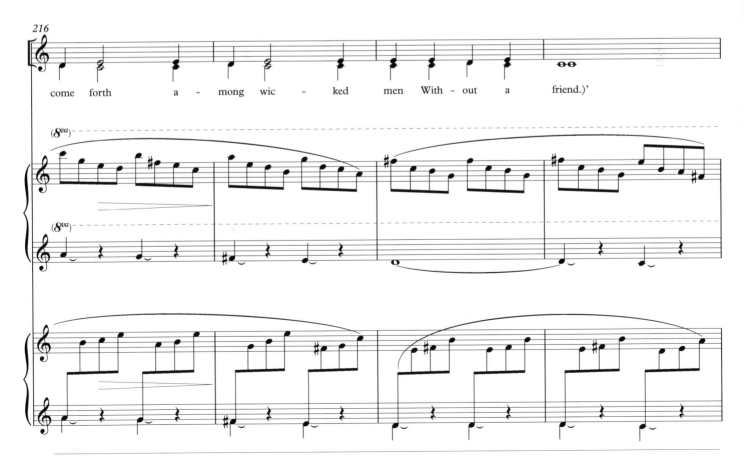

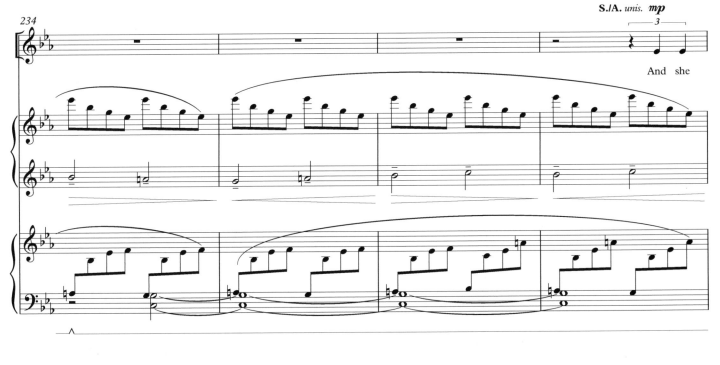

And she

reached out her hand, De — sir — ing to be near — er.

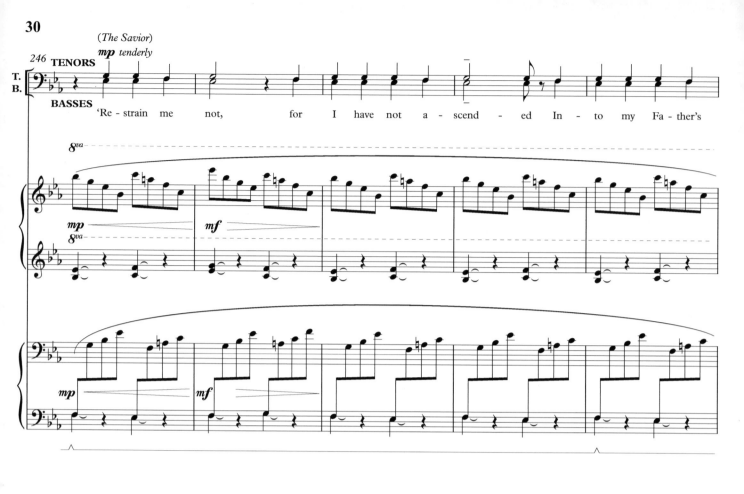

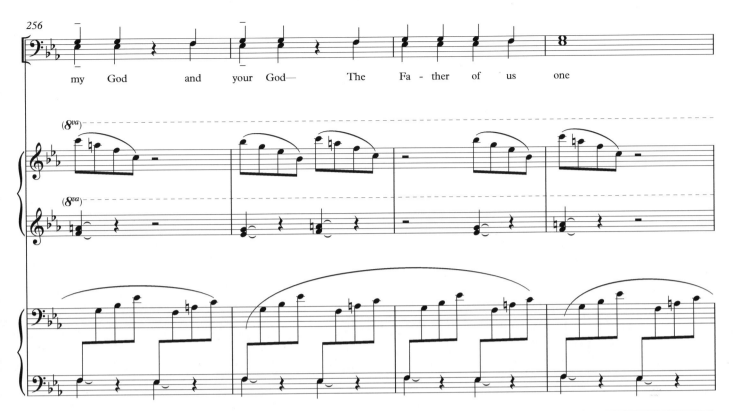

my God   and   your God—   The   Fa - ther   of   us   one

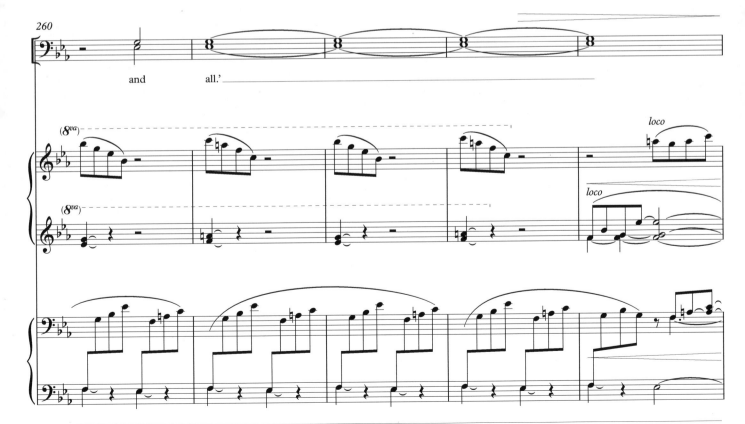

and   all.'

these were i - dle tales to those who doubt - ed.

When James - 's mo - ther went—

mp

Ped.

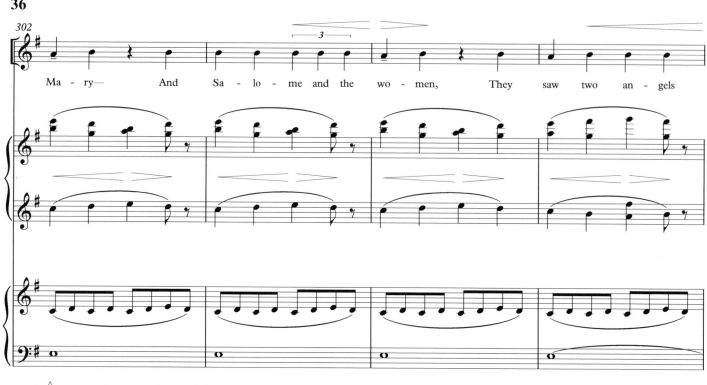

Ma - ry— And Sa - lo - me and the wo - men, They saw two an - gels

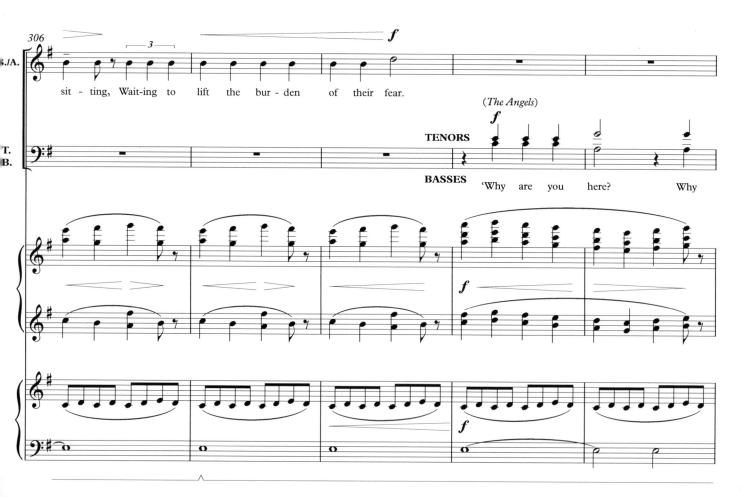

S./A.

sit - ting, Wait-ing to lift the bur - den of their fear.

(The Angels)

TENORS

BASSES

'Why are you here? Why

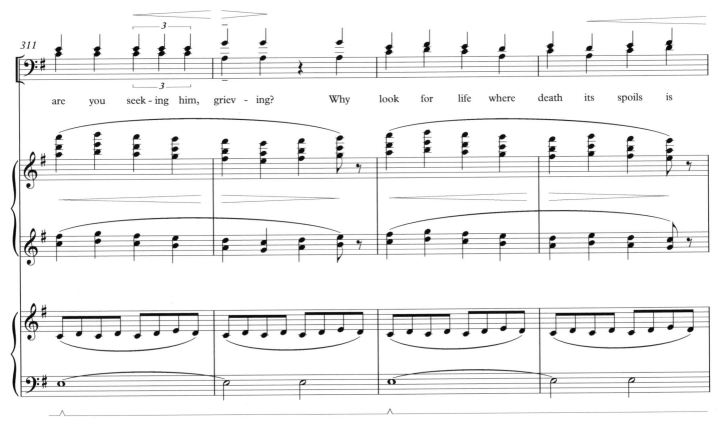

are you seek-ing him, griev - ing? Why look for life where death its spoils is

keep - ing? Come see where he was sleep - ing, Then go and tell he has ris - en, And

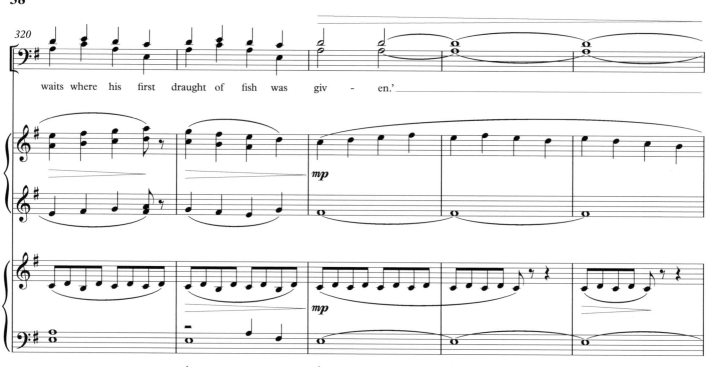

waits where his first draught of fish was giv - en.'

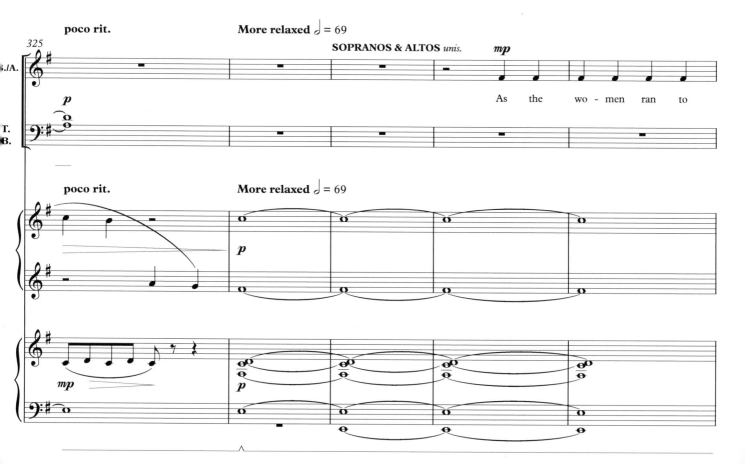

poco rit.　　More relaxed ♩ = 69

SOPRANOS & ALTOS *unis.*

As the wo - men ran to

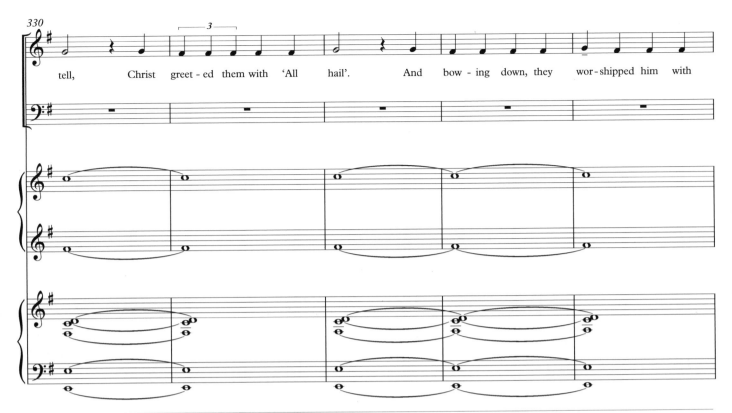

tell, Christ greet-ed them with 'All hail'. And bow-ing down, they wor-shipped him with

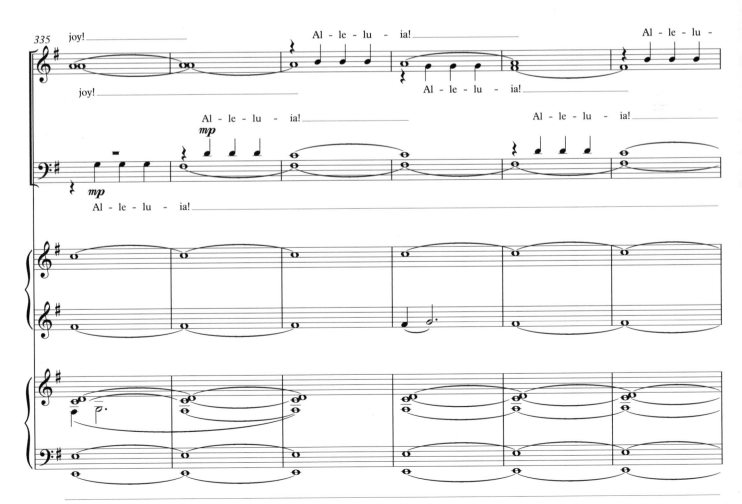

joy! Al - le - lu - ia! Al - le - lu -

joy!

Al - le - lu - ia! Al - le - lu - ia!

Al - le - lu - ia!

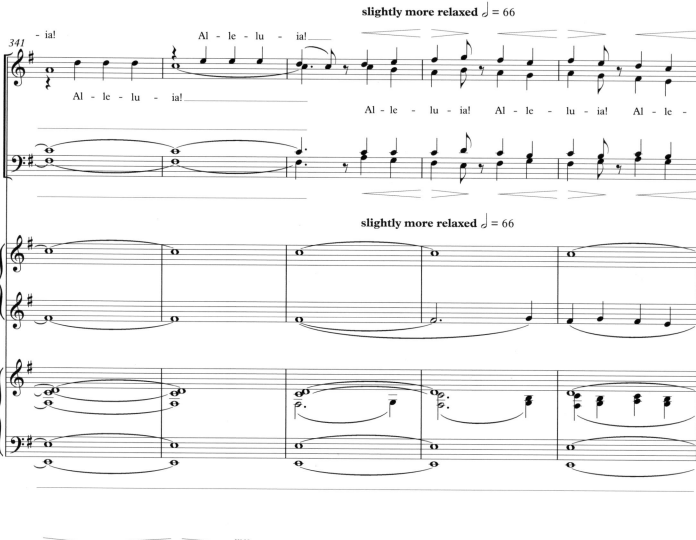

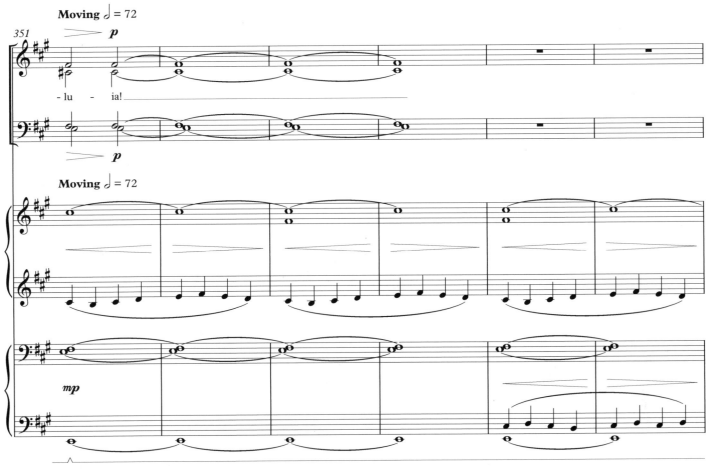

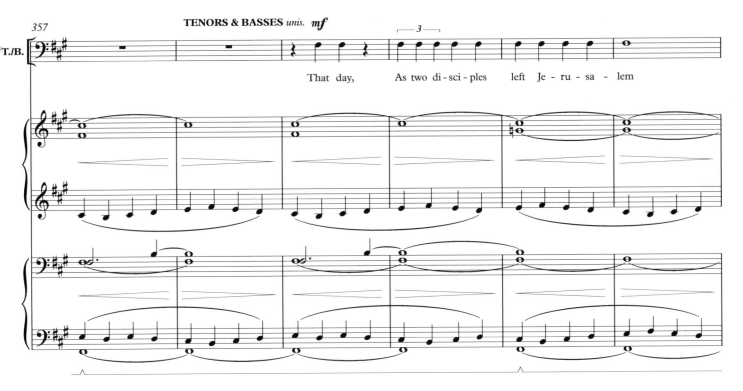

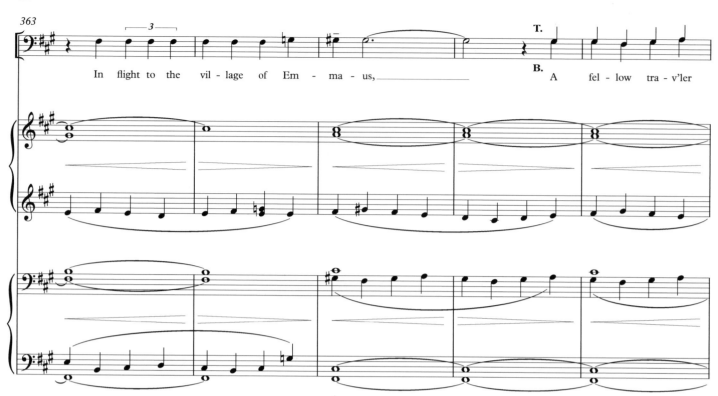

In flight to the vil - lage of Em - ma - us,_____ A fel - low tra - v'ler

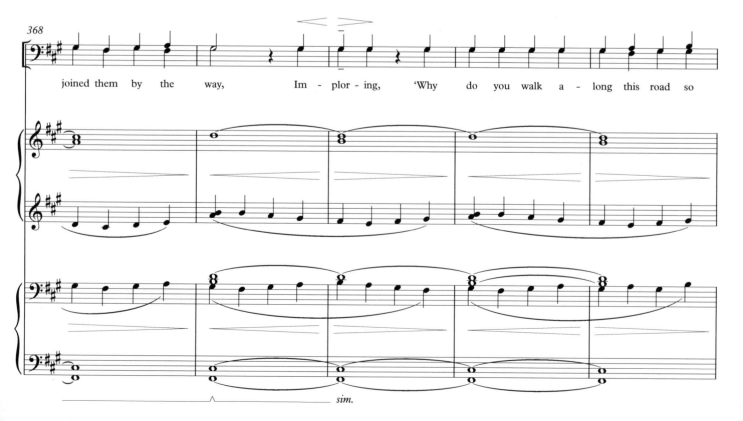

joined them by the way, Im - plor - ing, 'Why do you walk a - long this road so

373

unis.

sad?' _____ And they mar-veled that he was un-a-ware. 'Have

378

you not heard that Christ has been con-demned and cru-ci-fied? We trust-ed he was the

one who would re - deem all Is - ra - el. But thieves did steal his bo - dy, And

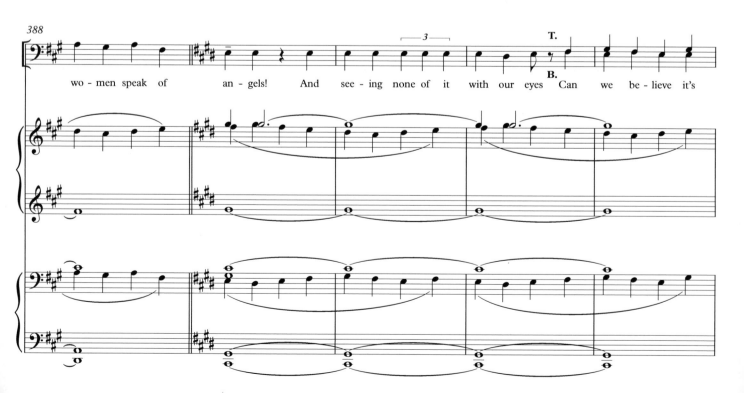

wo - men speak of an - gels! And see - ing none of it with our eyes Can we be - lieve it's

true? Good man, then what can we do but weep And sor-row through and

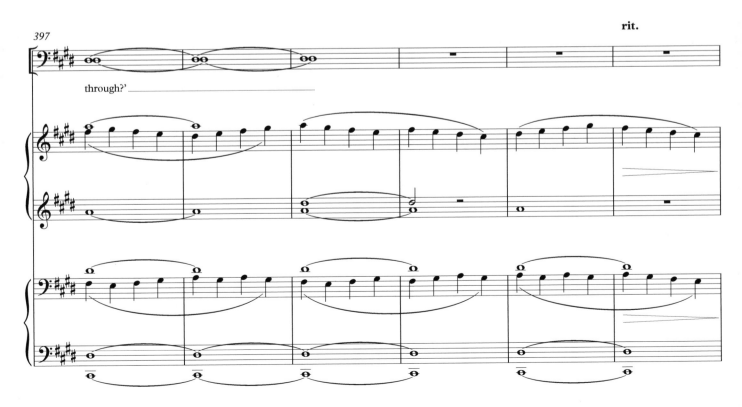

through?'

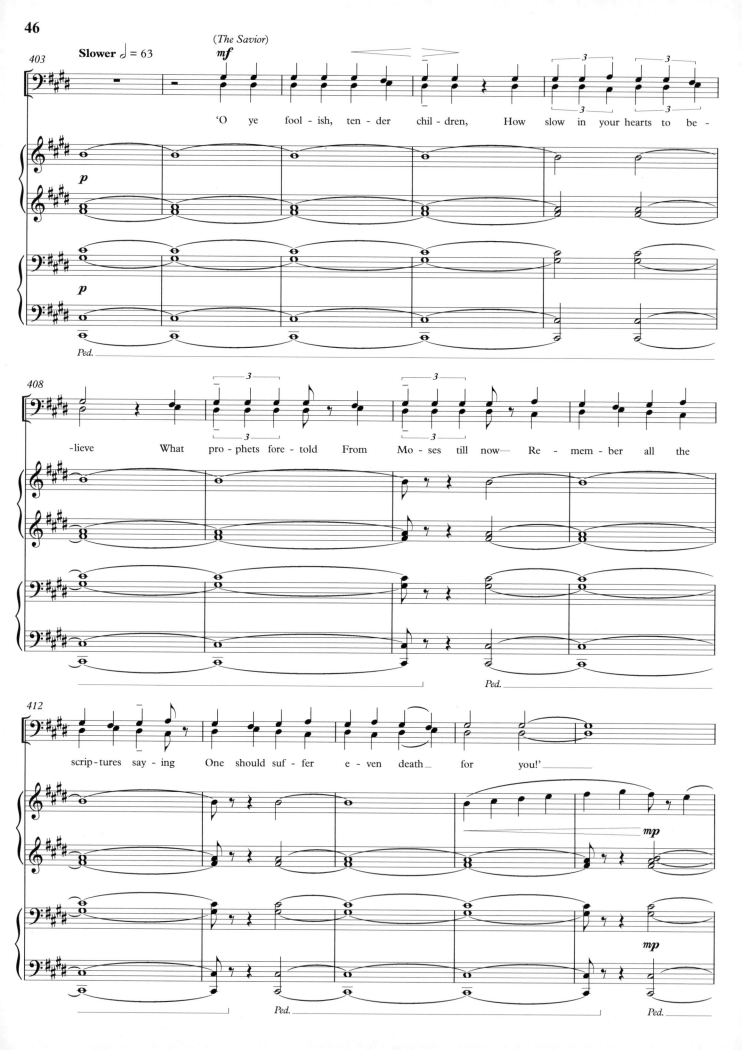

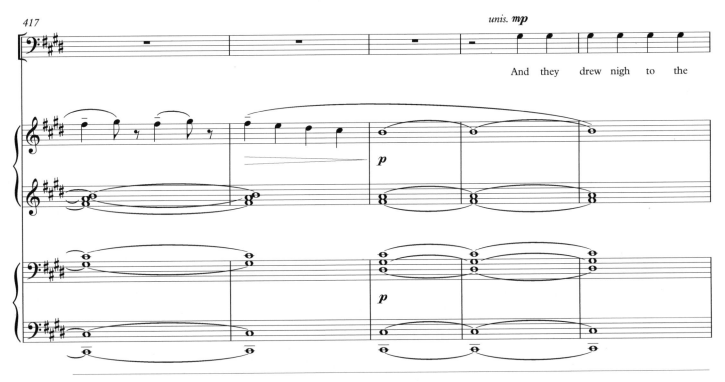

And they drew nigh to the

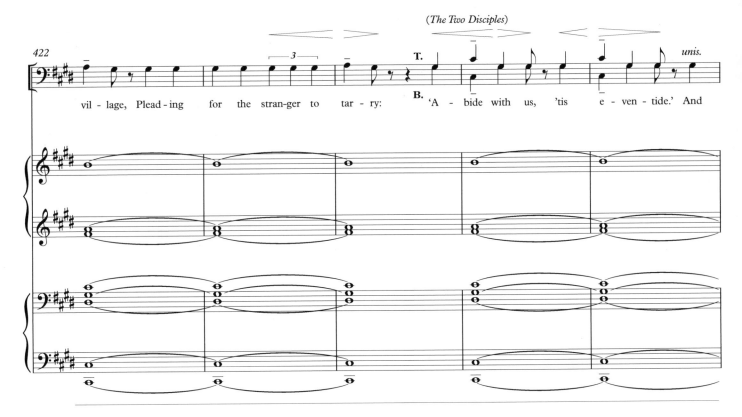

vil - lage, Plead - ing for the stran - ger to tar - ry: 'A - bide with us, 'tis e - ven - tide.' And

(The Two Disciples)

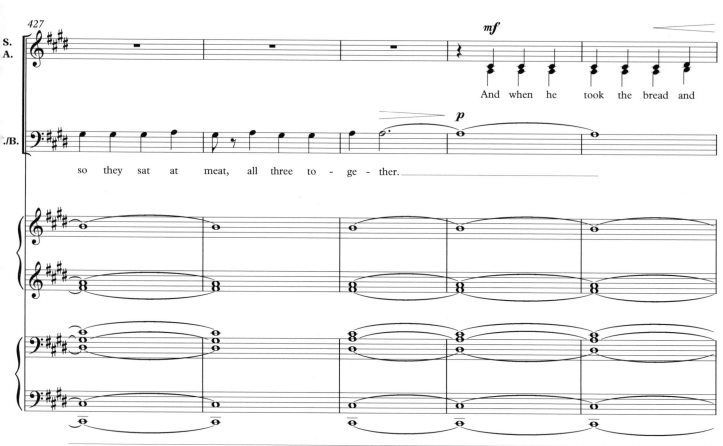

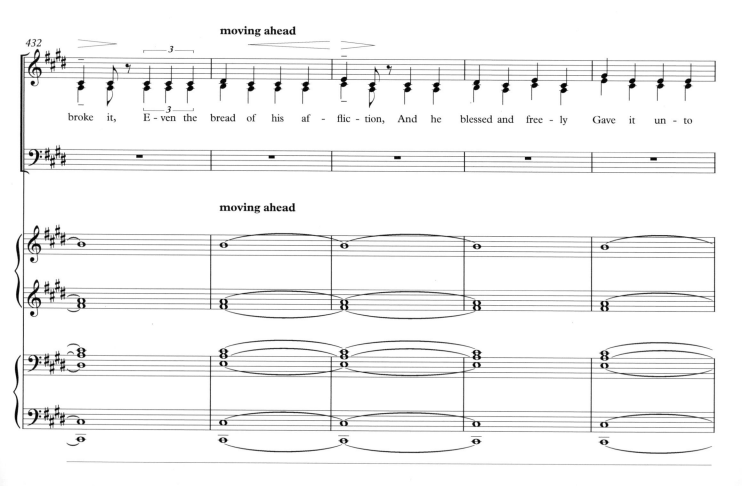

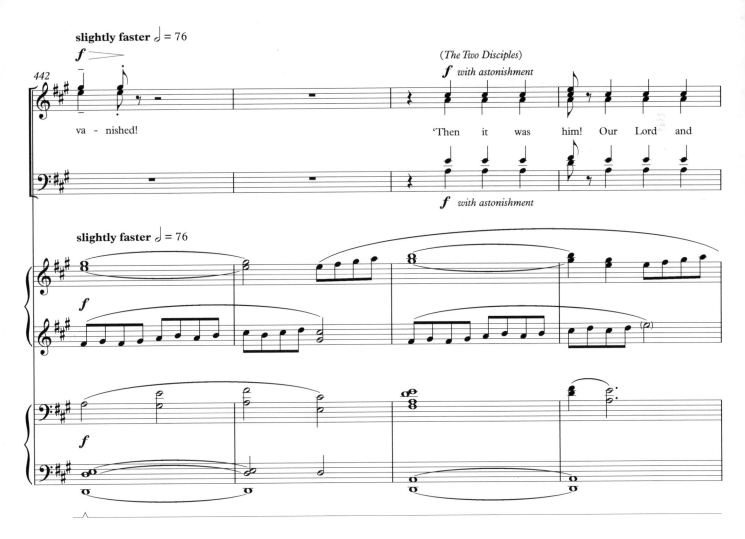

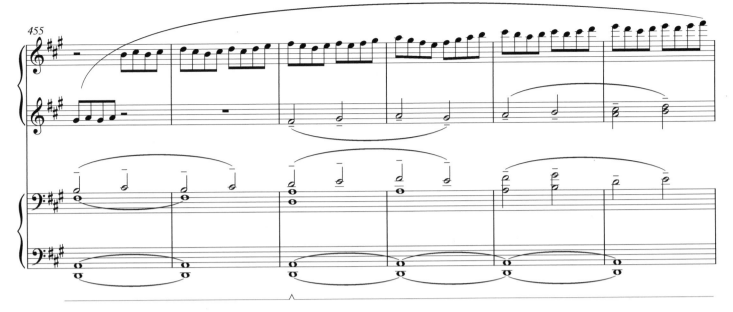

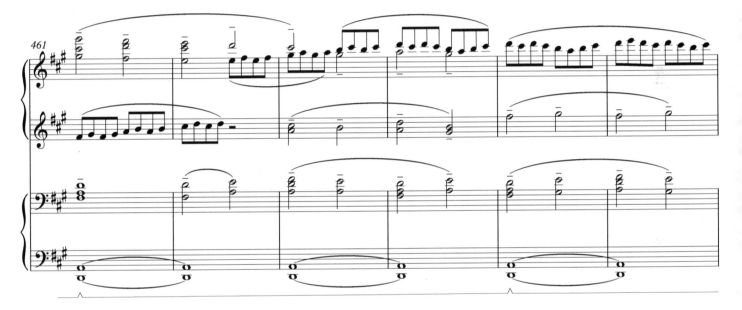

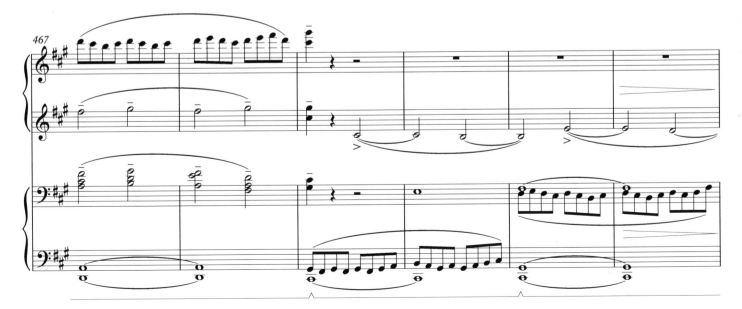

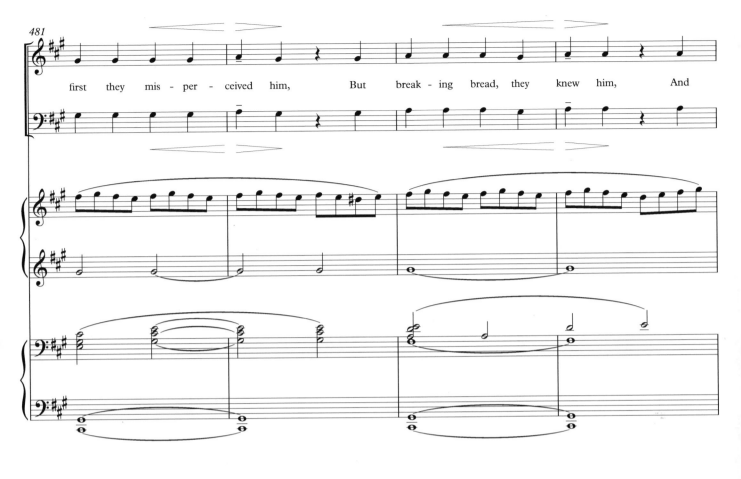

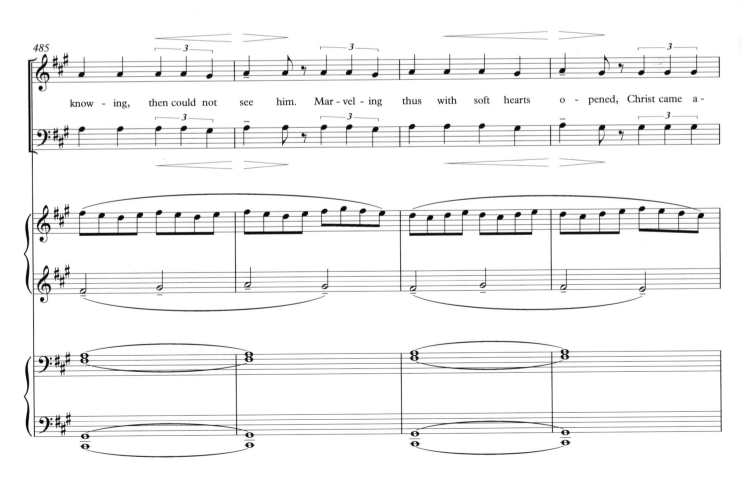

ghost! And trust - ing not their hearts But eyes in - stead, They yet be - lieved but

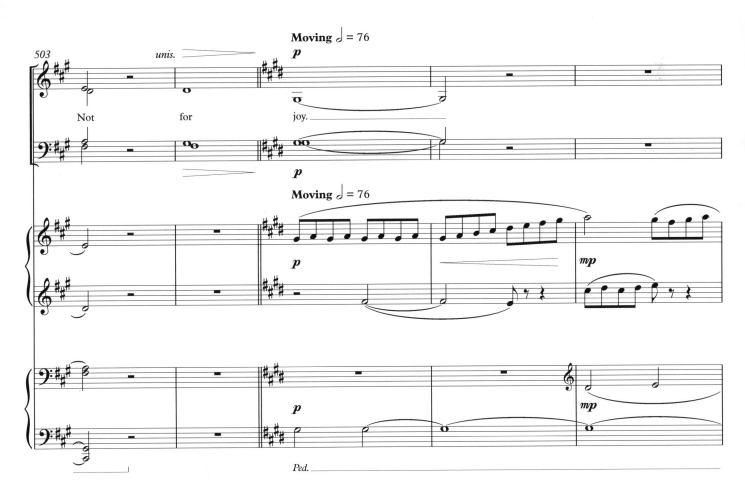

Moving ♩ = 76

Not for joy.

SOPRANOS & ALTOS *unis.*

Thus, in their fear-ing, The me-mo-ries of his be-ing Were

hid-den from them, And wi-thered in them, Un-til they heard him say — ing:

TENORS & BASSES *unis.* (The Savior)

'Why are ye trou-bled? What thoughts a-rise in your hearts? Be-

ten - der his wounds, He rea - died them to hear his sweet com -

slightly more relaxed ♩ = 69

(The Savior)
p

- mand:⎯⎯⎯⎯⎯⎯⎯⎯⎯⎯⎯ 'Be ye

(The Savior)
p

- mand:⎯⎯⎯⎯⎯⎯⎯⎯ 'Be ye wit - ness - es of these things,⎯⎯⎯

(The Savior)
p

'Be ye wit - ness - es of these things,⎯⎯⎯

(The Savior)
p

'Be ye wit - ness - es of these

540

wit - ness - es of these things, _____ be ye

_____ be ye wit - ness - es of these things, _____

be ye wit - ness - es of these things, _____

things, _____ be ye wit - ness - es of these

544

wit-ness-es of these things, _____ be ye wit-ness-es of these

_____ be ye wit-ness-es _____ of these

be ye wit-ness-es _____ of these

things, _____ be ye wit-ness-es _____ of these

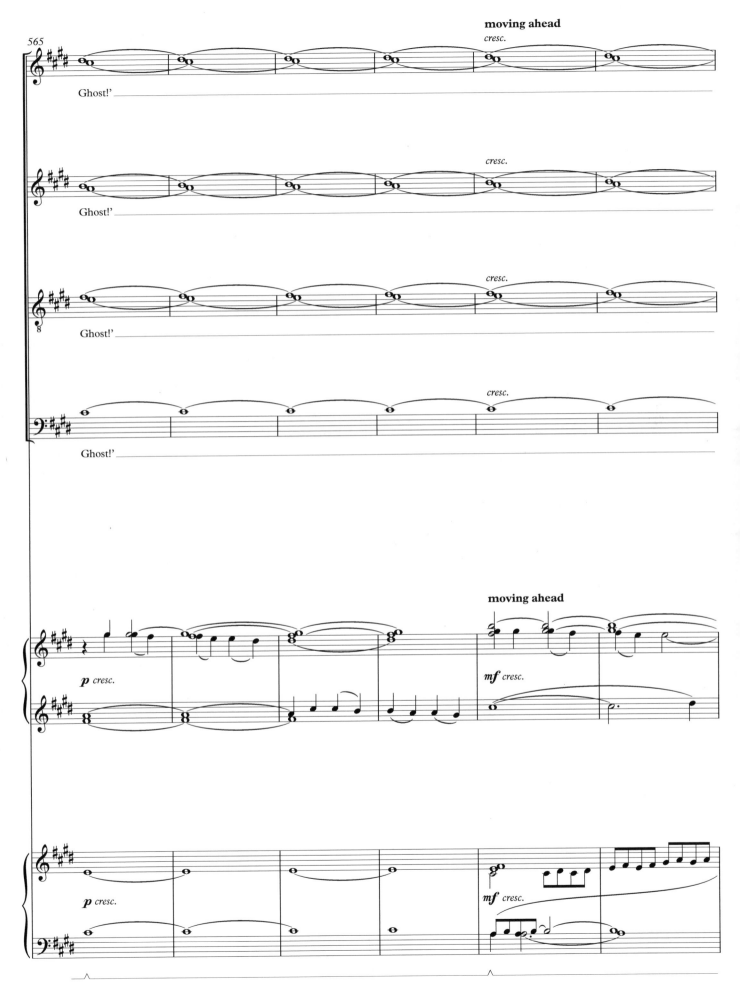

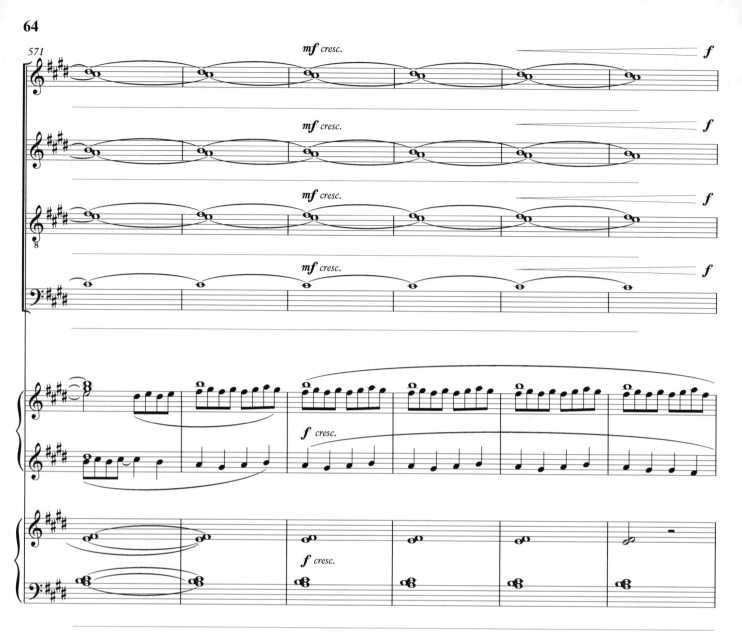

Moving, with settled tempo ♩ = 76

SOPRANOS & ALTOS *unis.*

But Tho - mas dis - be - lieved, For he saw not. And

since he had not be - held Christ, What wit - ness could he then bear? And

589

slightly more relaxed ♩ = 66

S./A.

eight days hence, to him and more Christ came:

(The Savior)
mp with reassurance

T.
B.

TENORS

BASSES

'Peace be un-to you. My peace I give un-to

slightly more relaxed ♩ = 66

mp

mp

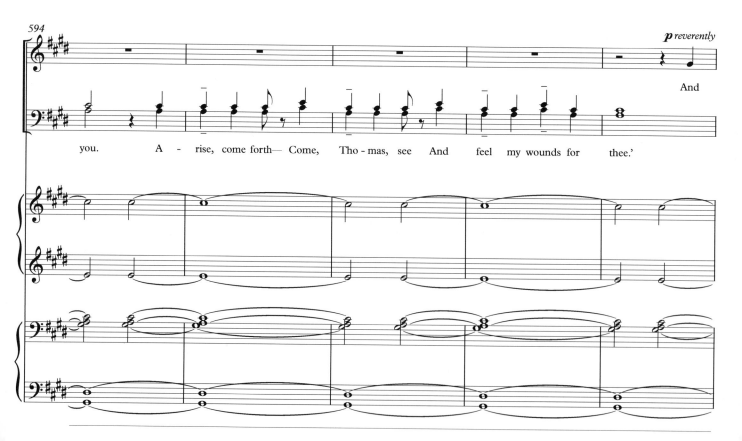

594

p reverently

And

you. A - rise, come forth— Come, Tho - mas, see And feel my wounds for thee.'

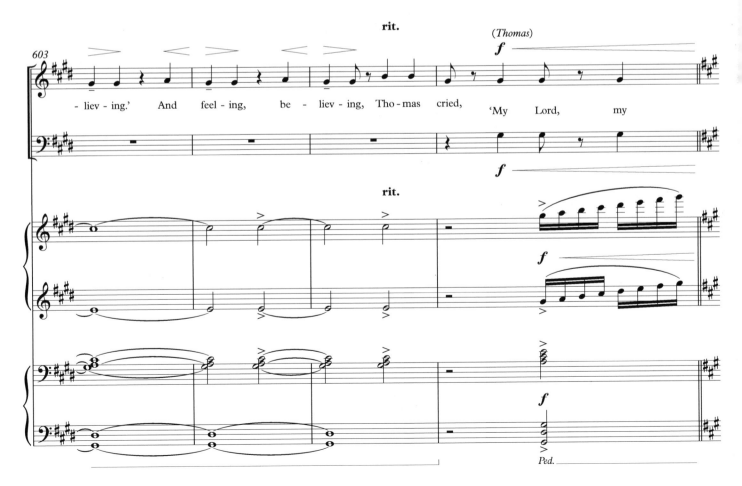

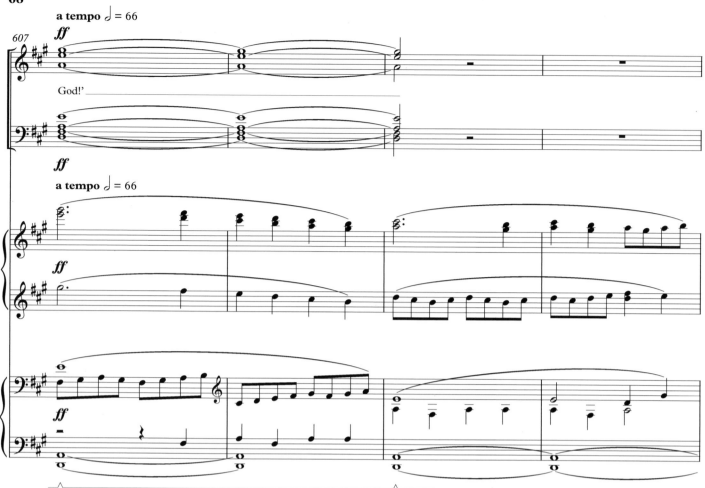

God!'

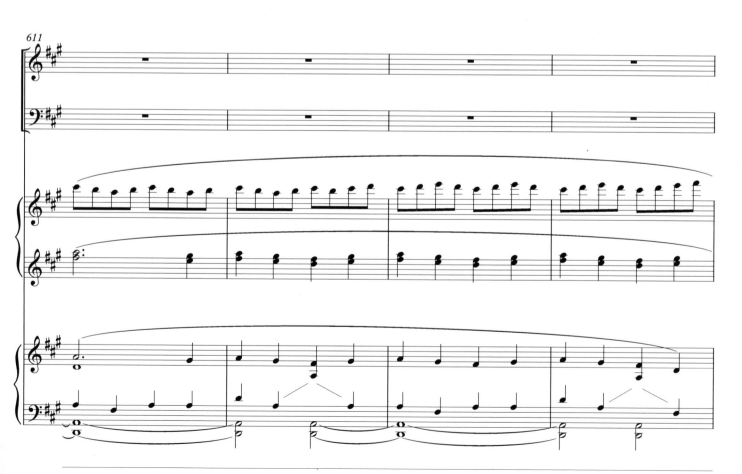

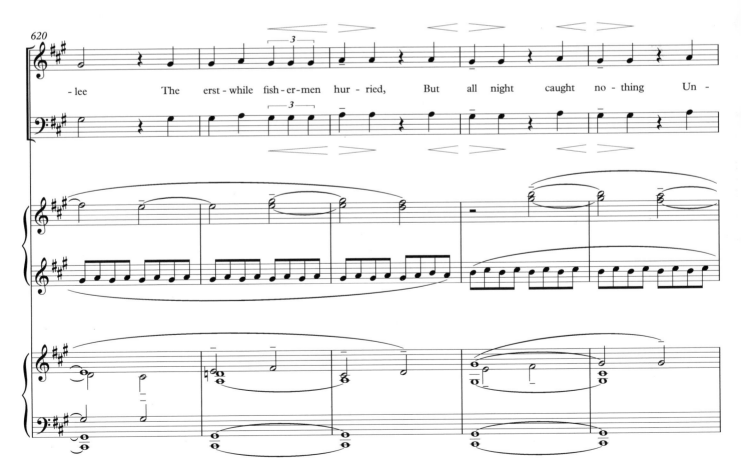

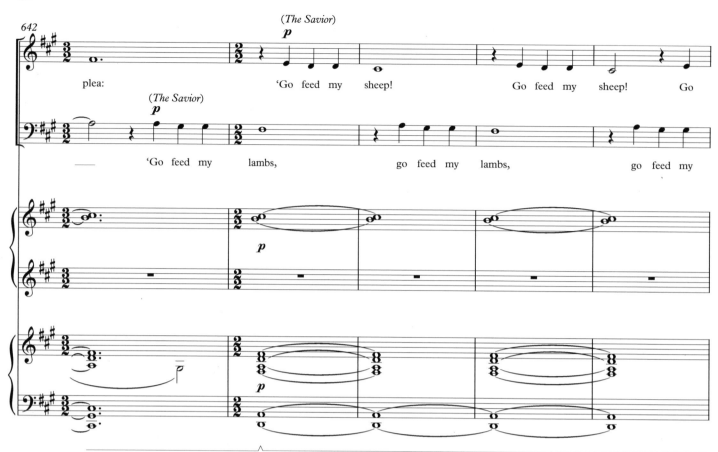

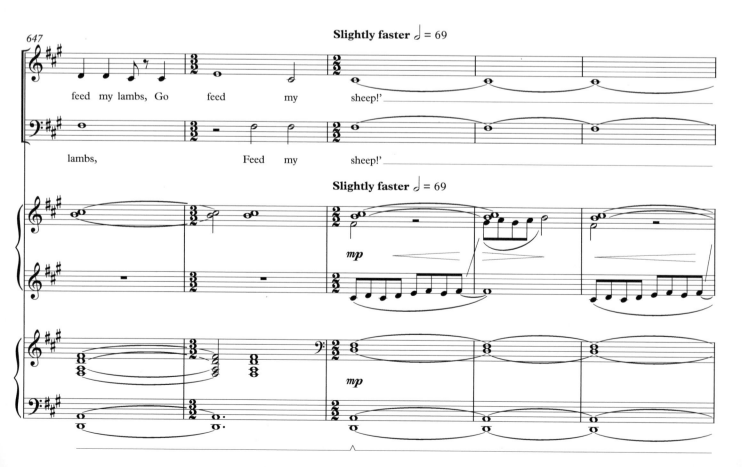

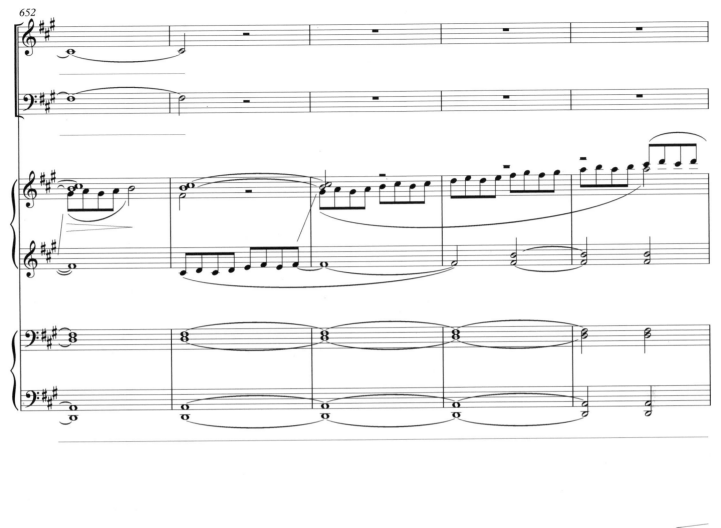

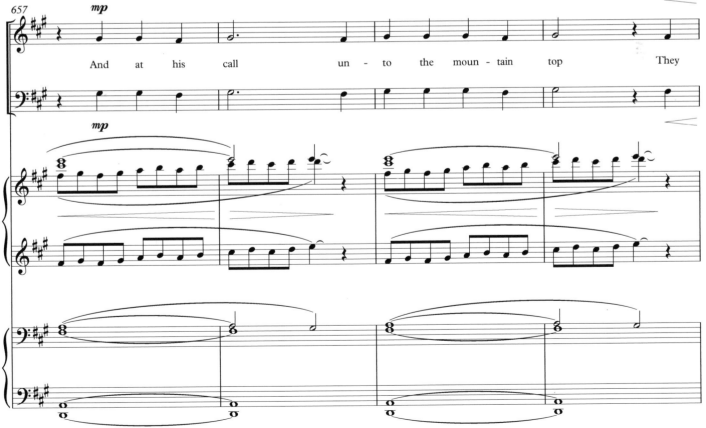

And at his call un - to the moun - tain top They

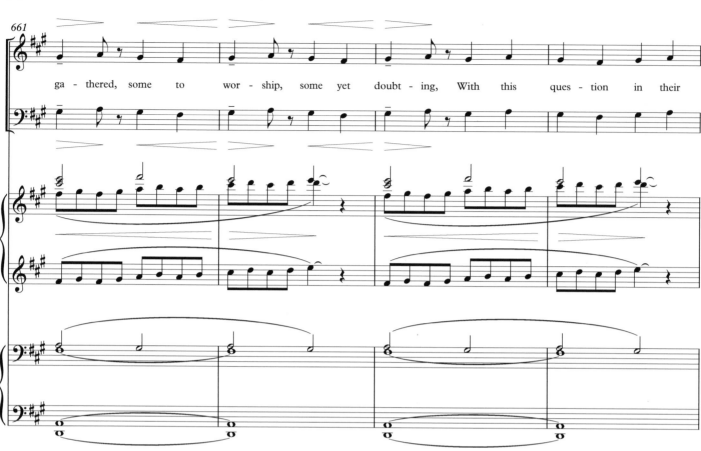

ga - thered, some to wor - ship, some yet doubt - ing, With this ques - tion in their

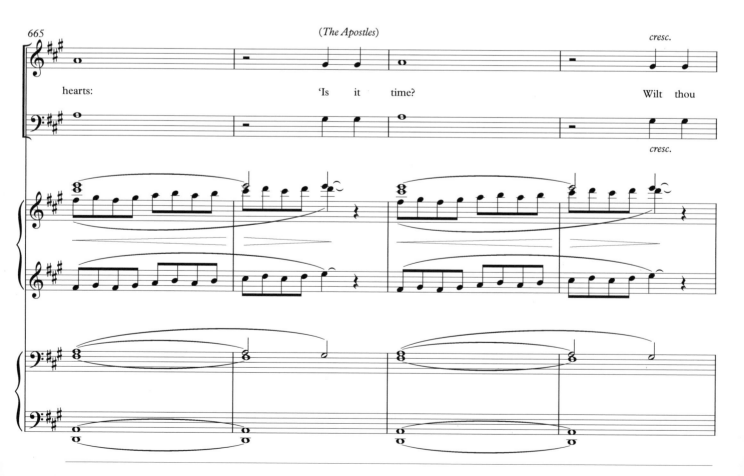

(The Apostles)

hearts: 'Is it time? Wilt thou

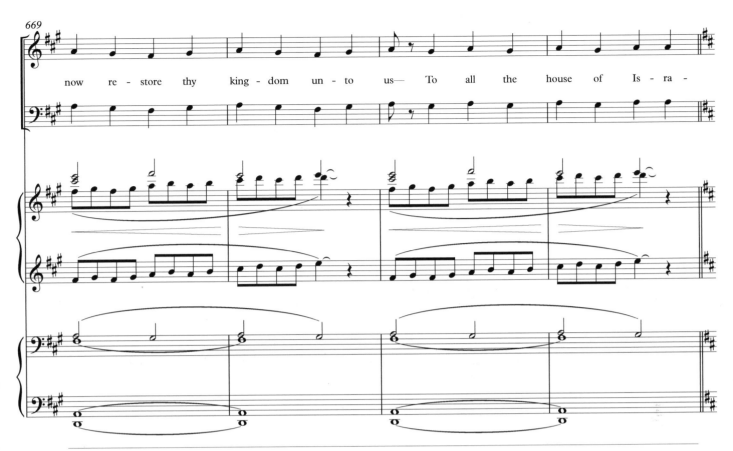

now re - store thy king - dom un - to us— To all the house of Is - ra -

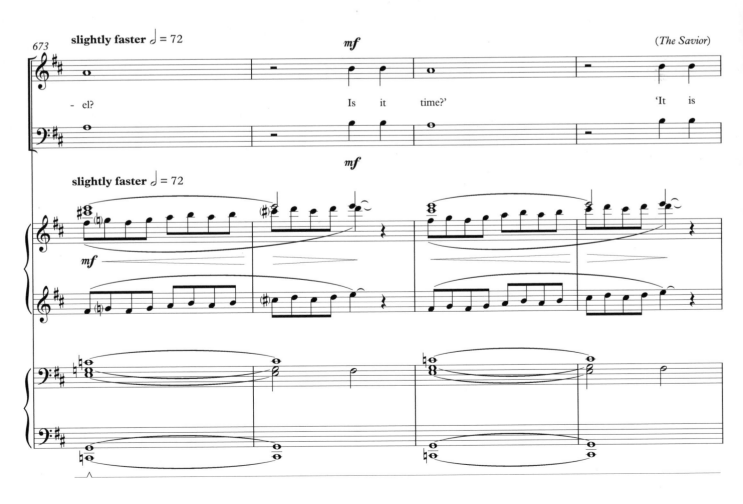

slightly faster ♩ = 72   *mf*   (*The Savior*)

- el?   Is it time?'   'It is

yet re - ceive his pow'r When soon the Ho - ly Ghost shall come up - on you.

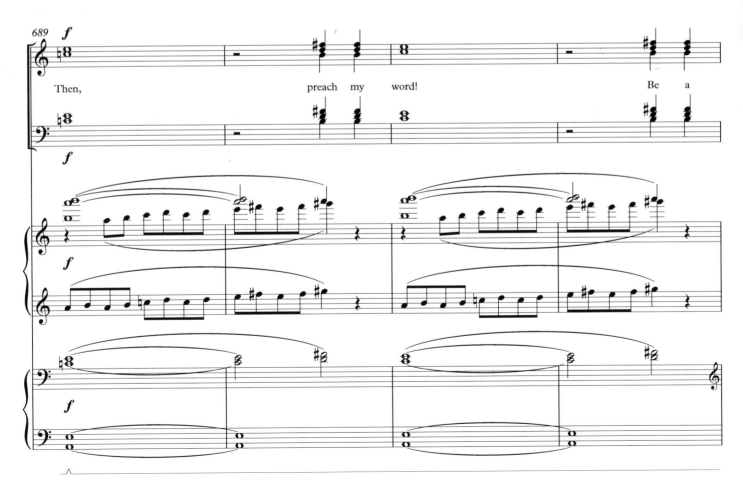

Then, preach my word! Be a

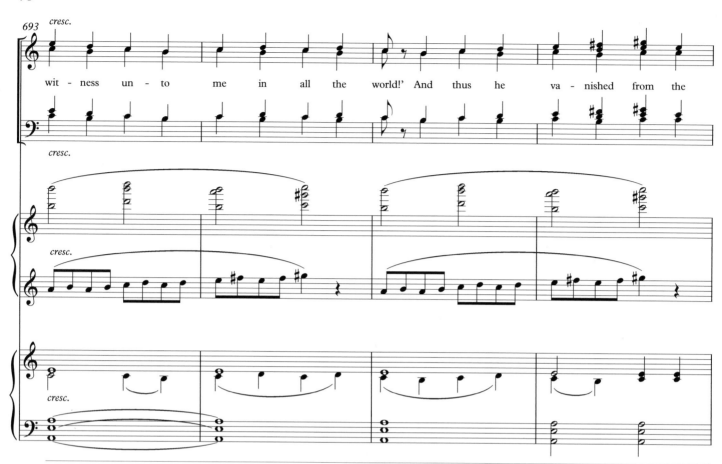

wit - ness un - to me in all the world!' And thus he va - nished from the

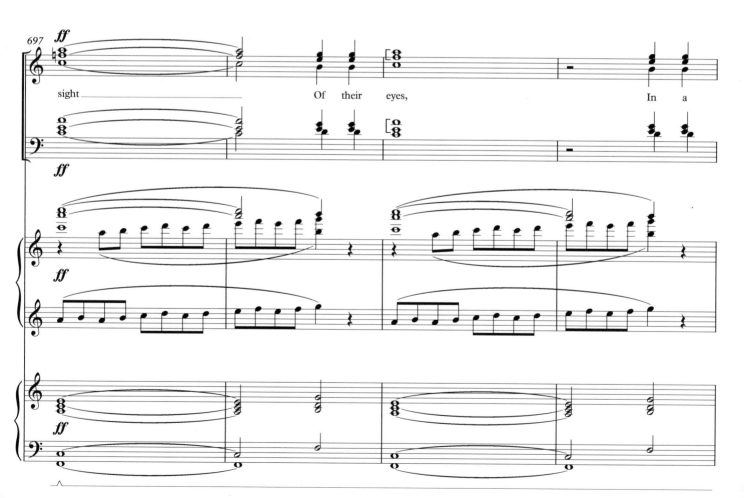

sight _____ Of their eyes, In a

cloud. Yet still they did yearn to see Till two

Relaxing tempo

dim. (*The Angels*) *unis.* **mp** *with awe*

an - gels asked, 'Why gaze up and grieve? For your

dim. **mp** *with awe*

Relaxing tempo

dim.

dim.

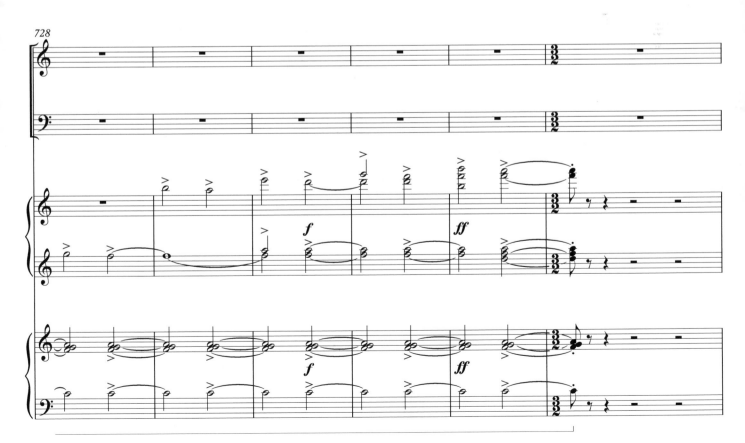

al - way, al - way,

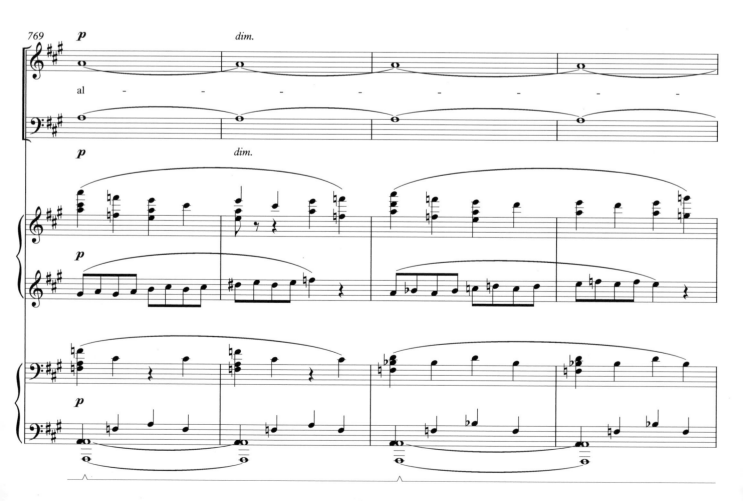

al - - - - - - - -

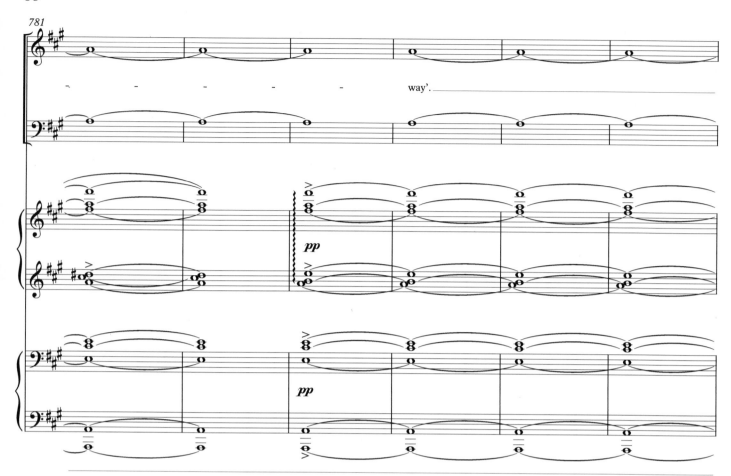

way'.

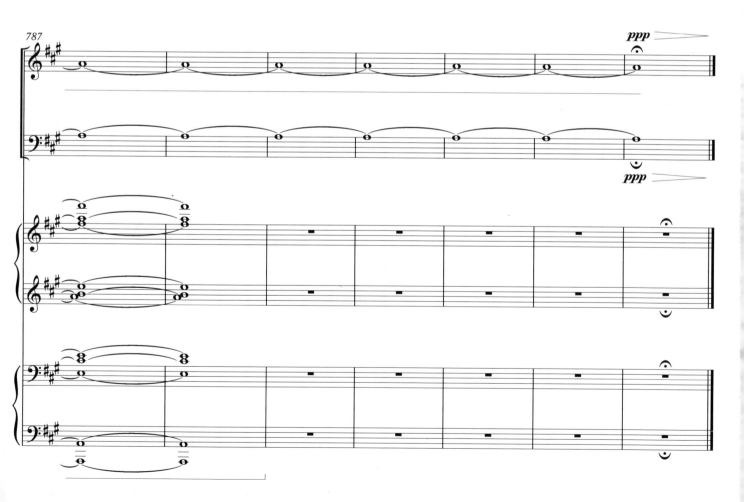